The Christian life is a journey, from loneliness and despair to companionship and joy, from sin and rejection to repentance and acceptance. The journey takes time and effort, but oh, the rewards!

Join Dr. Thereasa Ball on a journey of heart and soul, the journey of abundant life.

The Journey of Abundant Life

By Dr. Thereasa Ball

Published by BOTR Press, LLC
Poplarville, MS

All rights reserved. No part of this book may be used or reproduced by any means, graphic, electronic or mechanical, including photocopying, recording, taping or by any information storage electrical system without the written permission of the author except in the case of brief quotations embodied in critical articles and review.

All scripture quotations are King James Version unless otherwise indicated.

Copyright 2021
by Dr. Thereasa Ball

Published by BOTR Press, LLC
Poplarville, MS
www.BOTRPress.com
ISBN: 978-1-7378103-0-8

Cover photo courtesy Portia Ball Spann
Graphics by BOTR Press, LLC

The Journey of Abundant Life

By Dr. Thereasa Ball

Contents

Dedication 1
Forewords 3
    Min. Lynn Vonciell Morris, MSRP 6
    Dr. Charles Despenza, Chancellor 8
    Dr. Johnnie Ball, Apostle 10
Introduction 11
What Does Salvation Mean to You? 19
Cast Out of the Garden 21
    Action points for the reader: 24
Finding a Way Back 25
    Action points for the reader: 29
The Role of Faith 31
    Action points for the reader 33
Grace and Repentance 35
    Actions points for the reader 41
Closing the Gap to God 43
    Action points for the reader 49
Sanctified to God's Glory 51
    Action points for the reader 63
The New Path 65
    Action points for the reader 66
Prayer of Salvation of Abundant Life 67
Biography of Prophet/Dr. Thereasa Ball 69

Bibliography 71

Dedication

The Journey of Abundant Life is dedicated to my husband, Dr. Johnnie Ball, and our seven beautiful children, John I. Ball, Jonathan K. Ball, Portia Ball Spann, Casey Ball, Kimberly Ball Hudson, Josiah E. Ball, Keturah Ball-Harness and all of my grandchildren.

I pray that you will use this book as a guide to bring you and your family into an abundant life with our Heavenly Father, Jesus Christ and the Holy Spirit. I have thoroughly enjoyed writing this book and I hope that you will enjoy reading it and may it bring to you life, peace, joy and happiness. May God continue to bless and keep you and may He shine his light and love upon you always.

Dr. Thereasa Ball

Forewords

Foreword

The more we learn, the more we realize that we need to continue learning. This statement represents the epitome of the concept that what we know about the Holy Spirit does not scratch the surface of what we will learn about the Holy Spirit.

Dr. Ball meticulously carves out and dissects meanings and revelations that continuously guide us to the knowledge and love for God and his son Jesus Christ who left us with Holy Spirit to lead and guide us into all truths. Under her leadership, we come to know that we are the anointed.

It is not necessary to ask the anointing to come in a place. The anointing is already present because we are the anointed. We have the power to change the atmosphere. We have the power to speak to a situation and command it to obey.

With all of this, despite the challenges that we face as Christians, there is a still small voice that reminds us that we must forgive. To hear her say, "how would Jesus respond?" immediately resets our hearts towards our heavenly Father.

There is a constant reminder that facilitates compassion and walking in someone else's shoe to empathize with their plight and immediately forgive.

Our communion with God through prayer must be constant. As we move and navigate this thing called life, we must make our requests known to God. When we are in harmony with the will of the Father, His will leads to open doors, rivers that flow, and an open heaven on earth that will undoubtedly lead others to Christ.

HE must get the glory.

Min. Lynn Vonciell Morris, MSRP

Foreword

The Journey to Abundant Life is a most effective reference workbook about salvation. Dr. Thereasa Ball with her details balanced by her calm relaxed style of writing, has produced a comprehensive yet easy to read book. This book is only possible because of her experiences in ministry and as a lecturer, as well as her commitment to Christian education.

Here acknowledged that this natural life will one day end, is to ask the question "is there possibly more?" And to consider hearing about a Book that has been printed and read more than any other book in the world as being a source of knowledge about life. We need a copy or to attend where ever this book is being talked about. The Holy Scriptures.

In this workbook are given fragments of the spirit of questions, and answers, and doctrinal references to the question "What Does Salvation Mean to You?"

As its content speaks to having been cast out of the garden, trying to find a way back, holding on to faith, and in time being offered the understanding of grace, and repentance which helps to close the gap to God, being sanctified to the glory we find the new path, "The Journey to Abundant Life."

This workbook is such a bright light of day breaking through to a grassy path we have walked enclosed by a canopy, a forest of life's endeavors to find so much more when salvation has meaning to you as outlined by Dr. Ball.

As you begin turning the pages, your spirit is lifted with the spirit of God between the canopies of the different forests of this life to a more abundant life. Between these pages, we find a crowned rainbow of an outward expression of God's covenant (to hold back some of the overwhelming tears of our life's endeavors) to offer a working knowledge of salvation by Dr. Ball…a much-needed additional reassurance found in this workbook.

Dr. Charles Despenza, Chancellor
Christian Bible College of Southeast Louisiana

Foreword

I've always been fascinated with geography, history, and man's ability to navigate the earth. I am a child of the sixties; when paved roadways become highways, and highways widen to become interstate networks, travel was made easy. My fondest memories are of sitting in the back seat of the car tracing the trip to poppa's house with a multifold road map, watching for road signs, milestones, and wondering how the moon was able to keep pace with us no matter where we travel. Excited to discover with pinpoint accuracy the progress achieved from following the direction of the map and strictly observing the highway signs, city landmarks, mileage markers, detours, road hazards. Speed limits, warning signs, rest areas, service stations, hospitals, motels, signs are announcing destinations of cities, towns, bridges, and sharp curves all strategically placed along the traveler route to ensure a safe, comfortable, worry-free journey.

The Journey of Abundant Life is a spiritual road map designed to lead one to keep believers on a path that ensures Abundance of life. Dr. Thereasa Ball has created a simple, concise, easy-to-read workbook of essential foundational steps (Salvation, Grace, mercy, divine favor, etc.), which lead to a deeper, more meaningful relationship with Our Heavenly Father and His Creation. Dr. Ball's use of Holy Scripture reminds us that we are not on this journey alone. God orders the steps of a Good man: Jesus is the Way; no man comes to the Father, but by Him, Holy Spirit is your comforter, joy, and peace as we travel the narrow PATH that leads to eternal life.

This workbook is a handy tool for anyone in ministry. Pastors can prepare new members, and teachers have a training resource for students of all ages with the *Journey to Abundant Life* workbook. As an evangelical tool, new believers gain a critical understanding of The Father's plan of Salvation.

Dr. Thereasa Ball flows in the prophetic anointing with an ear sensitive to the Voice of God. The message of this workbook is timeless, practical, and life-changing. Please share it with someone; it will start them on a Journey of Abundant Life.

Dr. Johnnie Ball, Apostle

Christian Embassy Fellowship

Christian Bible College of Southeast Louisiana, President

Introduction

The Journey of Abundant Life will help you to determine what salvation means to you.

Salvation means different things to many people. Salvation can be viewed as one being saved from anything that may harm you or bring danger to your physical, emotional, financial and spiritual life.

This book will help you to engage in the ultimate journey to abundant eternal life through God the Father who created us. You will experience many dimensions as you travel through *The Journey of Abundant Life*.

Adam's disobedience separated us from God, but Jesus Christ reconciled us back to God through faith, grace, repentance, restoration, sanctification and glorification. The pathway in

The Journey of Abundant Life is a rewarding and a fulfilling life. It will bring us back into relationship with our Heavenly Father.

Once we have established our relationship then we need to fellowship with Him on a daily basis because He is in us and we are in Him.

Salvation is a gift from God, not earned but given to us because the Father loved us so much that He sent his son Jesus Christ to die not for us but as us. He shed his blood that we can have eternal life. If we accept him in our hearts we will never die. When we leave this earthly body, we will fall asleep and wake up in the arms of God in Heaven, but we will still be alive and live forever.

Some will not experience falling asleep on this earth. They will be taken up in Heaven like Elijah and Enoch. The Bible states, "Elijah was taken up in a chariot of fire (2 Kings 2:3-9) and "Enoch walked with God and he was not; for God took him" (Gen 5:21-24).

As we believe and have faith in Jesus Christ, He assured us that He would ask the Father to send us the Holy Spirit. The Holy Spirit will never leave us nor forsake us, but He will comfort, teach us and bring all things back to our remembrance.

We are sanctified for God's glory and now we reign here on this earth in our Terrestrial (earthly) body. When we no longer need this earthly body, we will inherit our Celestial (above the sky and Heavenly) body.

Let us walk down that pathway into The Journey of Abundant Life

THE JOURNEY OF ABUNDANT LIFE

The Journey of Abundant Life is a rewarding life fill with love, joy, and peace from our Heavenly Father. Our Father is a Spirit and we were all made in his image, therefore, we are spirits too. He birthed us spiritually in this world to activate his love. We loved him because He first loved us and because of Him we can love others around us. He sent the Holy Spirit to teach us unto all truth, comfort us when we are lonely, hopeless, the Holy Spirit gives of comfort and guide us in the path of righteousness (St. John 14:26, 15:13, 15:26).

The Father has given us the Seven Spirits of God to help us travel through this journey:

1. The Spirit of the Lord to mandate us for position to take dominion on this earth and to have the same power, son-ship and ruler-ship that He and his son Jesus Christ have.
2. The Spirit of Wisdom equips us for position, teaches us the skillful use of his knowledge and reveals God's justice, judgment and his mercy to us.

3. The Spirit of Understanding prepares us for position that we may get understanding as to why we use what he teaches us from the revelation of his word and how to teach others.
4. The Spirit of Knowledge empowers us for position. The Holy Spirit gives us instruction how to apply his knowledge to our life. His knowledge helps us to access his Kingdom realm of Heaven and translate it to the earth.
5. The Spirit of Counsel prepares us for position to resolve Kingdom issues and commune with God. The Spirit of Counsel teaches us how to rule and allow us to have ruler-ship on this earth.
6. The Spirit of Might reveals us for position to come into the supernatural realm of God. The Spirit of Might shows us how we can do the works of God in his Kingdom, dominion on the earth and seated in heavenly places with Christ (Eph 2:6). God rules and so do we.
7. The Spirit of the Fear of the Lord gives us accountability of holiness and majesty. The Spirit of God brings us into God's intimate reverence of who He is. We reverence God because He is sovereign, and He grants us the ability to travel down His path of abundantly life.

St. John 10:10 states, "Jesus came that we might have life, and that they might have it more abundantly." The journey is a process that we go through to assure us that we have life after death. This process grants us access in Christ through confession, repentance, faith, mercy, grace, sanctification and glorification.

Let us take The Journey of Abundant Life together.

What Does Salvation Mean to You?

When you consider "salvation," what do you think about? Do you have a clear picture in mind or are your thoughts filled with a myriad of images?

The word "salvation" carries many shades of meaning. For a drowning person, it may mean a life preserver or a lifeline. A starving man may find salvation in a crust of bread. A drink of water may save someone suffering from thirst.

Salvation can be physical, emotional, financial or spiritual. For a Christian, salvation is an intensely personal experience connecting them to God through his Son. In this book, we will take an in-depth look at the journey to abundant life through spiritual salvation and the importance of doctrine in understanding the path God laid out for us.

This book is not a lecture to be read at an emotional distance. It is intended as a guidebook to help you along the way to a meaningful experience with the One who loves you best. You'll find questions in each section; your answers will help you gauge where you are now in your spiritual relationship and help you to move closer to God. Start a Salvation journal and add to it as you gain insights from the text and answer the action questions. You'll create a lasting tool to help you stay on track.

Cast Out of the Garden

At the start, human beings lived in the Garden of Eden, in harmony with God and his Creation. Can you imagine how wonderful the situation was? How blessed they were?

But it didn't last. In the Garden of Eden, man was separated from God because of his disobedience. When Adam and Eve sinned, they broke the relationship and needed to be restored to God. Their restoration took place through repentance and grace.

Just like Adam and Eve, we need to be restored back into fellowship with God because of our sins. Salvation is a gift from God and this gift can only be received through faith, grace, repentance, restoration, sanctification, and glorification.

It is crucial for us to understand the importance of salvation. Let's take a deep look at what it means.

Salvation is the entrance to our relationship with God.

"Salvation denotes deliverance, preservation of material, and temporal deliverance from danger and apprehension of the spiritual and eternal deliverance granted immediately by God to those who accept His conditions of repentance and faith in the Lord Jesus. It is to be obtained through confession that Jesus Christ is our Lord. For this purpose, the gospel is the saving instrument of the present experience of God's power to deliver from the bondage of sin."[1]

---

[1] Vine, W.E., The Expanded Vines Expository Dictionary of New Testaments Words, (England by Oliphants, Marshall Pickering, 1940), p.988

When a person has received salvation, he will escape the wrath of God in the Final Judgment. Salvation allows him to be renewed and restored to the fellowship with God that he lost in the fall, and to be delivered from all the effects of sin. All the spiritual blessings, which come in Christ Jesus, will be bestowed upon us by His mercy and grace.

Titus 3:4-5 says:

"But after that the kindness and love of God our Saviour toward man appeared, not by works of righteousness which we have done, but according to His mercy He saved us, by the washing of regeneration, and renewing of the Holy Ghost."

Salvation is the result of our deliverance and the scope of what God has provided for us in Christ. We want to get back into the Garden with God.

Action points for the reader:

1) Have you experienced a "Garden of Eden" relationship with God in your life? If so, describe it.

2) What human weaknesses get between you and God?

3) Where are you in your relationship with God now?

4) Would you like your relationship to change? If so, where would you like it to be?

Finding a Way Back

In general, we are lost, helpless, and unable to save ourselves. The scale of sin blinds us and we need to be delivered from the resulting darkness. Salvation removes the scale from our eyes so we can see God's plan and purpose for our life. It allows God's plan and thoughts to be seen more clearly. Jeremiah 29:11 says, "For I know the thoughts that I think toward you, saith the Lord, thoughts of peace, and not evil, to give you an expected end."

We need to be saved from the penalty of sin. While we live under the penalty of sin, we have sinful ways, thoughts, and acts. The Bible makes it clear in Romans 3: 23 and other verses: we have all sinned and come short of the glory of God. Our pardon is through the gift of salvation.

Salvation is a gift from God that cannot be bought or earned. God gave us this gift through Jesus Christ. The gospel of St. John 3:16 says, "For God so loved the world, that he gave his only begotten Son, that whosoever believeth in Him should not perish, but have everlasting life."

In order to receive this gift, we must confess with our mouth and believe in our heart that God raised Jesus from the dead.

The Doctrine of Salvation is connected with Jesus the Christ.

"The worth of salvation depends on the worth of the Saviour. If He were sinful like every other man, His death could pay for no more than His own sins because the wages of sin is death. Just as the Passover Lamb was proven to be without blemish before it was slain (Ex. 12:5-6), our Lord was proven perfect and a sinless sacrifice for our sins." [2]

The gift of salvation is an eternal gift which keeps our mind and our heart satisfied. God gave salvation to us so that we can be assured He loves us so much that He prepared a place for us to come and be with him as our final resting place.

My husband gave me a gift. I was not there when he purchased it, I do not know where he bought the gift or how much it cost. By faith I can accept his gift or reject his gift. I believe that my husband loves me dearly and he will not give me anything that will harm or hurt me. I accept the gift in that spirit.

Spiritually, God is the giver of salvation and we must receive it by faith. God has given every man the measure of faith. It is faith if we believe and have confidence in God that His word is true. "Faith is belief and trust in and loyalty to God, complete trust, something that is believed

---

[2] Ryrie, Charles Caldwell, A Survey Of The Bible Doctrine, (The Moody Bible Institute of Chicago, 1972), p. 115.

especially with strong conviction without doubt or questions." ³

A person who is generous, intelligent, strong and healthy may find it difficult to accept salvation from God simply because of his own accomplishments in life. He must believe in God instead of his works. Ephesians 2:8-9 says, "For by grace are ye saved through faith; and that not of yourselves: it is the gift of God: not of works, lest any man should boast."

God will always honor His Word. "God communicates His thoughts through His Word. When He enables us to hear what He is saying to us by the Spirit, this creates within us the response of believing that what He is saying is true and directed to us." ⁴ Romans 10:17 says, "So then faith cometh by hearing, and hearing by the Word of God."

---

³ Webster, Merriam Inc., Webster's Ninth New Collegiate Dictionary, Springfield, Massachusetts, 1983), p. 446.
⁴ Beall, James Lee, Pastor and Marjorie Barber, Laying The Foundation, (Bridge Publishing, Inc. South Plainfield, New Jersey, 1976), p. 65.

When we hear God's Word and rely on His Word, we learn to trust Him. We will not lean to our own understanding.

Action points for the reader:

1) Offers of free gifts come from all directions. How do you judge the value of the offered gift?

2) How do you decide which gifts to accept?

3) Have you ever missed out on a gift because you didn't accept it? How did you feel about missing it?

4) What would you be willing to give to purchase your own salvation, if you could? What are you willing to give to accept the gift from God?

The Role of Faith

Faith must have an object of trust. The object may be a person: a friend, a relative, a coworker, a leader. It may also be a non-living thing, such as a chair.

Consider the trust you exhibit when you sit on a chair. It could be old. It might be a little fragile. The screws could be worn and wobbly in their holes. The upholstery may be thin, and a spring may poke through. It may break and collapse. But we still have faith as we sit down that the chair will hold us up. "It is not enough just to have faith, but we must put our faith in a trust-worthy object. How much faith we have or what kind of faith we have is not important. It is important who we have our faith in." [5]

---

[5] MacDonald, William, What The Bible Teaches, (Emmanus Correspondence School, Dubuque, Iowa), 1976, p. 40.

If we put our faith in Jesus Christ, He will never leave or forsake us, because of His trustworthiness. Faith is the first step in pleasing God. Hebrews 11:6 says, "But without faith it is impossible to please Him: for he that cometh to God must believe that He is, and that He is a rewarder of them that diligently seek Him."

We please God by remaining open to the truth of His word. The Holy Spirit will teach us the truth of God's Word and He will help us develop a firm conviction of what we believe. As we mature in faith, we no longer operate in unbelief. We will not be enticed to accept other doctrines because we form a commitment to God's Word, and He has established us in Him. Isaiah 7:9b says, "If ye will not believe, surely ye shall not be established." God wants to develop and make us perfect <u>in Him</u> through faith.

Action points for the reader

1) Can you think of some examples in your own life of putting your faith in things outside of your control?

2) Has your faith ever been abused by the person or thing you trusted? How did you feel when it happened? How did you recover your trust, if ever?

3) What evidence have you seen in your own life of God's faithfulness? Did you see it as it was happening or only looking back at events?

Grace and Repentance

God deals with us through grace. Jesus is described as the God of all grace. First Peter 5:10 says, "But the God of all grace, who hath called us unto his eternal glory by Christ Jesus, after that ye have suffered a while, make you perfect, stablish, strengthen, settle you."

"In the Old Testament, the word grace means to bend or stoop down in kindness to someone who is inferior. In the New Testament, the word grace means favor, good will, and loving kindness." [6]

God's grace – His unmerited favor – requires no labor. God shows us favor which we do not deserve.

The law requires justice, but grace finished that work on Calvary and served the sentence

---

[6]   ibid p. 35

for us. The law reveals the sin and grace reveals salvation. We are sinful; we have disobeyed God's law, but because of his mercy and grace, He continuously extends his love.

God's grace offers us salvation. "If we are going to be saved, it must be by God's grace because God is holy, and He will not overlook sin. Sin must be punished." [7] Grace brings us salvation. Titus 2:11 says, "For the grace of God that bringeth salvation hath appeared to all men."

Grace and salvation justify us and provide us access to God's throne. However, we must go before the Father with a humble and repentant heart.

Having a repentant heart means to experience godly sorrow. "For Godly sorrow worketh repentance to salvation not to be repented of: but the sorrow of the world worketh death," according to 2 Corinthians 7:10.

---

[7] MacDonald, William, What The Bible Teaches, (Emmanus Correspondence School, Dubuque, Iowa, 1976) p. 36

Repenting signifies we recognize we have sinned against God and we need forgiveness. We are repenting from dead works, because dead works break fellowship with God. Once our fellowship is broken, we lose our ability to serve Him.

In Isaiah 59:2, the prophet says, "But your iniquities have separated you and your God." (21st Century King James Version)

At this point, sin has caused a corruption in our character. The only way we can be restored is to repent and ask God for forgiveness. Repentance and forgiveness bring us back into fellowship with God. Each time we sin we must repent to be reconciled to God. Repentance causes us to turn away from sin and places us in a position to receive the Word of God. Through His Word He provides us His revelation of His love.

God's sovereign call draws men to repentance. Scripture is rich with references to the importance of the need for sinners to repent.

Matthew 9:13 says, "I am not come to call the righteous, but sinners to repentance." God uses the ministry of His Word to create repentance in the heart of man.

> "How when they heard this, they were pricked in their heart, and said unto Peter and to the rest of the Apostles, men and brethren, what shall we do? Then Peter said unto them, Repent, and be baptized everyone of you in the name of Jesus for the remission of sins, and ye shall receive the gift of the Holy Ghost." Acts 2: 37-38

True repentance will cause man to turn around and turn to God.

> "The word repentance in the Old Testament is "Naham", means to feel sorry, to lament, to grieve, to sigh, or to groan and "Shubh" means to turn back, to make a radical change in attitude toward sin and God. In the New

Testament, repentance means "Metanoia and Epistrepho". Metanoia expresses the intellectual and spiritual change which occurs when a sinner turns to God. The meaning of Metanoia is to have another mind or to change one's mind, attitude, and purpose regarding sin. It describes an inner turning around. Epistrepho indicates the distinct change, which results from repentance – a change of position in relation to God. Summarized as a spiritual transition from sin to God, from death to life."[8]

Our spiritual change occurs when we have a broken and contrite heart. If we are truly sorry for that sin and our heart is so broken in humility, we should not sin in that area of our life again because the purpose of repentance is to turn back and go in an opposite direction.

---

[8] Beall, James Lee, Pastor & Marjorie Barber Laying The Foundation, (Bridge Publishing, Inc.) South Plainfield, New Jersey, 1976), p. 12-13.

When we view repentance from an intellectual standpoint, we recognize repentance as a remorseful feeling of deep regret, of hopelessness and even despair. Having a remorseful feeling may not lead to constructive change, nor does it help us to believe in God, but it turns us against ourselves. We have a tendency to try and change ourselves. When we find no success, we experience despair and our emotions sometimes permit us to do ungodly things. Many times, our own efforts get in God's way.

Romans 7:5 says, "For when we were in the flesh, the motions of sins, which were by the law, did work in our members to bring forth fruit unto death." We cannot change ourselves without the Holy Spirit's work of regeneration. "Not by works of righteousness which we have done, but according to His mercy He saved us, by the washing of regeneration, and renewing of the Holy Ghost; which He shed on us abundantly through Jesus Christ our Savior," according to Titus 3:5-6.

Actions points for the reader

1) Can you think of a situation when you earnestly desired to repair your relationship with God, but weren't sure you could do it? How did you proceed?

2) How do you experience repentance in your life?

3) What actions do you take to maintain an attitude of repentance? What penitent habits have you formed?

4) Does repentance make you feel closer and more connected to God or in some way more distant? Why?

Closing the Gap to God

The fall of man separated us from God. The bridge across our separation is salvation. When we accept Jesus Christ as our Savior, He allows the Holy Spirit to guide, teach, and comfort us into all truth. We accept His truth; He becomes our Lord and personal Savior through salvation, and we give Him praise for our life.

God made us and shaped us in His own image. He provided redemption to us, to save us from the curse of the law. He redeemed us because we could not redeem ourselves. Jesus Christ paid the price for our sins. He delivered us out of darkness.

> "Redemption is one particular kind of deliverance. The word redemption comes from the marketplace. It is a

commercial term used to describe salvation as a business transaction. Redemption is the purchase of something that has been lost. It is the securing of a release by the payment of a ransom."[9]

In God's great mercy, He has given us new birth into a living hope through the resurrection of Jesus Christ from the dead. "The source of all true life spiritually as well as physically is the resurrection of Jesus Christ. The same Spirit who raised Christ from the dead also raises the Christian to new spiritual life. By the power of the Holy Spirit, resurrection produces regeneration."[10]

The new birth is essential to salvation and without it, there is no spiritual life. Either we are born-again Christians, or we are not Christians

---

[9] Ryken, Philip Graham, The Message of Salvation, Minister of Tenth Presbyterian Church, Philadelphia, Pennsylvania, p.91
[10] Ryken, Philip Graham, The Message of Salvation, Minister of Tenth Presbyterian Church, Philadelphia, Pennsylvania, p.147

at all. Jesus was in conversation with Nicodemus, a community leader, when He explained the necessity for spiritual rebirth.

> "Jesus answered and said unto him, Verily, verily, I say unto thee, Except a man be born again, he cannot see the kingdom of God. Nicodemus saith unto him, How can a man be born when he is old? can he enter the second time into his mother's womb, and be born? Jesus answered, Verily, verily, I say unto thee, Except a man be born of water and of the Spirit, he cannot enter into the kingdom of God. That which is born of the flesh is flesh; and that which is born of the Spirit is spirit."
> John 3:3-6

We cannot enter back into our mother's womb to born again physically; therefore, we must be born again of the Spirit.

It is essential that our minds be renewed. We cannot think like we did when we were lost. We have to cast down every high thought that goes against the will of God. Romans 12:2 says, "Do not be conformed to this world, but be transformed by the renewing of your mind, that you may prove what is that good and acceptable and perfect will of God."[11]

The evidence of the new birth in a born-again Christian will be a demonstration that he bears new fruit. We should possess the fruit of the Spirit (love, joy, peace, long suffering, kindness, gentleness, meekness, goodness, and faith). When we study the Word, it should fall on good ground. "All believers will bear fruit, Matthew 13: 7-8 says, and some fell among thorns; and the thorns sprung up and choked them: but others fell into good ground, and brought forth fruit, some a hundredfold some sixty fold, some thirty fold."[12]

---

[11] George, Elizabeth, <u>Following God With All Your Heart</u>, Growth and Study Guide, Harvest House Published by Harvest House Publishers, Eugene, Oregon 97402, p.73

When we were sinners, we lived a sinful and carnal life.

"The word carnal means to have the nature and characteristics of the flesh (or more simply, it means fleshly). To live carnally means to be characterized by things that belong to the unsaved. Carnal things can be money, material, lust and passions (Gal 5:19-24; 1 John 2:16), it can enslave (Romans 7:25; and it is nothing good (Romans 7:18)."[13]

When we walk in the Spirit, we do not have to fulfill the lust of the flesh, because when God redeemed us, we became justified through God.

In justification, a man receives a new personality.

"The meaning of justification is a divine act whereby an infinitely Holy God judicially declares a believing sinner to

---

[12] Ryrie, Charles C., So Great Salvation, Moody Publishers, Chicago, Ill., 1997, p.53
[13] Ryrie, Charles C., So Great Salvation, Moody Publishers, Chicago, Ill. 1997, p.54

be righteous and acceptable before Him because Christ has borne the sinner's sin on the cross and has become to us righteousness."[14]

Man is justified by faith. It is the declarative act that declares man righteous by the remission of the penalty.

The penalty for sin is death. That death can be a spiritual, physical, and eternal death. Romans 6:23 says, "For the wages of sin is death; but the gift of God is eternal life through Jesus Christ our Lord." If a man is to be saved, this penalty must first be removed. It was removed by and in the death of Christ, who bore the punishment for our sins in his own body on the cross. First Peter 2:24, says, "Who His own self bare our sins in His own body on the tree, that we, being dead to sins, should live unto righteousness: by whose stripes ye were healed."

---

[14] Unger, Merrill F., The New Unger's Bible Dictionary, Revised and updated edition, The Moody Bible Institute of Chicago, Ill., 1988, p.728

Justification is by the grace of God and through His grace we might be made heirs according to the hope of eternal life. Our justification is not because of something that we have done, but by God's mercy and grace. Man is not justified by the works of the Law but by the faithfulness of Christ Jesus. "The justified man is assured that he will be saved from the coming wrath of God (Roman 5:9), and he is also assured of glorification. (Matthew 13:43; Romans 8:30; Gal 5:5)."[15]

Action points for the reader

1) In our judicial system, a convicted prisoner can receive a pardon and have the penalty of the crime wiped away. How do you compare God's gift of salvation to a judicial pardon?

---

[15] Thiessen, Henry Clarence, Lectures In Systematic Theology, Wm. B. Eerdmans Publishing Co., Grand Rapids, Michigan, 2006, p.279

2) Jesus saw you as worthy of His sacrifice on the cross. Do you feel worthy? Why or why not?

3) How do you respond to God's gift of grace?

4) How can you share the story of God's grace with others?

Sanctified to God's Glory

Sanctification is defined as being set apart. We are set apart from the world and sanctified to God. It also means "the act of God in setting us aside for Himself and is related to the idea of the holiness of consecrated things used only for God's services."[16] Before our salvation we ran away from God and toward sin. After salvation, we move toward God and away from sin. Our spiritual victory or defeat depends on the direction we are pursuing.

The Bible frequently uses the term sanctification. In the Bible its primary meaning is a state of consecration to God. Both "the Greek word Hagiazo and the Hebrew word Kaudash means to sanctify, to consecrate, or

---

[16] Young, Douglas G, <u>Young's Bible Dictionary</u>, Tyndale's House Publishers, Inc., 1989, p. 475

denote a person or thing to a particular, especially to a sacred use."[17]

Sanctification has three phases, positional, progressive, and perfect. "We have a past, a present, and a future as believers in Jesus Christ."[18] When we receive Christ, we are seated with him in heavenly places. We are positioned with him and we no longer see ourselves in the past tense, but we become in the present. We must also see ourselves as saints of God. We gain victory by knowing who we are in Jesus Christ and we must progress according to our position. We should take on the characteristics of Christ daily and know that we are not perfect because of sin in our life, but that we can work towards perfection in Him.

We are exalted in Jesus Christ. Spiritually, we know who we are in Him. We no longer see ourselves in the past tense as sinners, but we

---

[17]   Finney, Charles G., Rev, Finney's Systematic Theology, 1878 Edition, Gospel Truth Ministries, Tustin, CA, 1966, Lecture 37, Sanctification
[18]   Evans, Tony, Totally Saved, Moody Publishers, Chicago, IL, 2002, p. 131

become in the present as Saints of God and we should see ourselves as God see us.

Our growth should always progress in Him. Progressive sanctification involves acting in accordance with our position. This is the present tense of sanctification concerning our daily conduct of Christians behavior. Areas in our life need to be worked out with fear and trembling.

We need to cleanse our soul of all defilement of the flesh in order for us to embrace holiness. God is holy and we should be holy. We are holy in position, but not in our practice because we are still in our flesh. We are not perfect because of sin in our life, but we should work towards perfection in Christ. Progressive sanctification means that we are now telling sin what to do and where to get off instead of sin dictating to us.

Perfect sanctification will be completed one day when we reach our eternal destination. We will be present with the Lord. We will no longer need these earthly bodies, we will have our glorified bodies. Everything will be perfect. No more headaches, worries, or tears regarding the cares of this world.

When God calls us home, we will be raised as a complete sanctified and glorified Saint. We do not have to wonder about salvation and life after death as other religions. "The Buddhist idea of salvation is believing that hell is a kind of purgatory perhaps, a lackluster place for souls that are ill-defined, that never found their real purpose for being."[19]

Christians have a place prepared for them in Heaven with God. Jesus told the dying thief on the cross that he would be with Him in paradise (Luke 23: 40-43). That was a promise of immediate glory in God's presence. "It won't matter where your body is or what condition it is in, because when God calls you home, you will be raised as a perfectly sanctified and glorified Saint for Heaven."[20] Sanctification is a

---

[19] Killinger, John, The Changing Shape Of Our Salvation, The Crossroad Publishing Company, New York, NY, 2007, p. 90-91

[20] Evans, Tony, Theology You Can Count On,

two-sided truth that includes set apart from worldly things to set apart for holiness and worship to God.

The Glory of God is so infinite that our finite mind cannot comprehend, but through His wisdom and knowledge we can learn of His love, power and His manifested glory. The word glory means, "presence, accompanying power, and brilliance manifested by the appearance of a deity or divine spirit. The presence of the Lord God, His Son or His Holy Spirit. It also indicated a witness of the favor and grace of the Lord."[21]

God's glory demonstrates to us who He is. His divine power is above any and all power on the earth and in heaven. Everyone will bow before Him one day because He is Lord of lords and King of kings. We show God's glory in our life by being obedient to the Holy Spirit in everything He tells us to do.

Moody Publishes, Chicago, IL., p. 786
[21]   Price, Paula A. PH.D., The Prophet's Dictionary, Whitaker House, New Kensington, PA. 15068, p. 237

We don't do things on our own. The chain of command is from the Father through Jesus Christ, from Jesus Christ to the Holy Spirit, and from the Holy Spirit to us. John 17:4 reports Christ said, "I have glorified thee on the earth. I have finished the work which thou gavest me to do." "The more we know Christ, the more we reflect His glory.

The glory that the Spirit imparts to the believer is more excellent and lasts longer than the glory that Moses experienced."[22] Moses knew and obeyed God because Christ had not come yet, but when Christ came and died for our sins, we accepted and knew Him and learned all of the miraculous things God did through Him.

When we go to Heaven we will not be in our fleshly body, we will be in our glorified body. "Glorification is the third stage of Christians development. The first being justification, then sanctification and finally glorification.

---

[22] C:/ProgramData/Wordsearch, The Handbook of Bible Application, p 2

Glorification is the completion, the consummation, the perfection, the full realization of salvation".[23] The glorification of God's creation in human species in which He expresses his image and likeness of Himself is His Terrestrial glorification. The word "Terrestrial" means earthly.[24] The Lord put us here on earth so we could live here and have all the things we need for our comfort and joy.

His original plan for man was to live forever on the earth. Man was endowed with the glory of God to take dominion over the earth, but because of his disobedience he lost the provision, the perfect state of health and the right standard with God. Thank God, Jesus restored man to his rightful place with God through His redemption blood through salvation.

---

[23] Https://en.wikipedia.org/wiki/glorification, Wikipedia, The Free Encyclopedia, p 3
[24] Www.dawnbible.com/1961/6109tbs2.htm, Topical Bible Study, God's Plan for Man- Lesson VI, p.1

- We glorify God on this earth by surrendering to His perfect will. To serve Him with every fiber in our body.
- We glorify God by being obedient to what He commands us to do. To put Him first in everything and to take full advantage of every opportunity He gives us in ministering to His people.
- We glorify God by being thankful for what we have instead of complaining what we don't have.
- We glorify God by having a joyful heart when life dictates to us unfortunate circumstances. We can rest in Him because our burdens are the Lord.
- We glorify God through our prayer life and the compassion we show toward His people.
- We glorify God through our spiritual life by allowing the Holy Spirit to direct our life in the way it should go.
- We glorify God by our character on how we conduct ourselves daily to others through

our walk and our conversation measured by the Word of God that they may see the fruits of the Spirit of love, joy, peace, kindness, gentleness, meekness, long suffering, goodness and faith.

- We glorify God by loving those that hate us, falsely accusing us of doing wrong, spreading discord among the saints, and even being hostile toward us when we preach the truth of His Word.
- We glorify God by being Christlike.

The Bible tells us to lay up treasures in Heaven. This treasure is not earthly, but it is God's Celestial glorification. "The word celestial means above the sky and heavenly."[25] We have a beautiful prize waiting for us as we give up those earthly things that corrupt us and are delivered from every evil work.

We have to continue to reach, press and hold on to obtain what is stored up for us in Heaven. The apostle Peter reminds us we are called, "To an inheritance incorruptible and undefiled, and

---

[25] Www.dawnbible.com/1961/6109tbs3.htm, Topical Bible Study, God's Plan for Man-Lesson V11, p.1

that fadeth not away, reserved in heaven for you. (21st Century KJV)" The things on this earth that was gain to us we count lost for Christ.

God's creation groans and travails for the manifestation of the sons of God at the second coming.

"The creations know that it is in bondage until this happens. But when this takes place, the corruption to bondage will be lifted and the creation will be set free and so obtain the glorious liberty of the children of God. The significant mark of this glorification for both creation and human body is freedom."[26]

We will be free from the suffering of this world and the weakness of our flesh and temptation of the enemy. When Jesus ascended to Heaven, He assured us the Promise of the

---

[26] Ramm, Bernard, Them He Glorified, Wm. B. Eerdmans Publishing Company, Grand Rapids, Michigan, p108

Holy Spirit. We are sealed with that promise. We looked forward to the new earth and new Jerusalem of the Eschatology Era. One day God will perfect what He started in the beginning before the fall of man.

"The individual acts of our now-salvation are eschatological in character. Justification is eschatological in that it anticipates the complete vindication of the believer in the end-time when all things shall be made new, the palingenesis of all things. The word palingenesis is used for our present new-birth, but also for the rebirth of all things. Sanctification is eschatological in that it looks forward to the perfection of all things. That which sums up the eschatological realization and fulfillment of our justification, our regeneration, and our sanctification is our end-time glorification"[27]

Christ will come and receive us to Himself. The Bible says those who are dead in Christ will rise first. The Church will be caught up to meet Him in the sky. The devil will reign for seven years. Those that are left here that have not confessed Jesus Christ as their Savior will be given another chance for salvation.

When a bride waits at the altar for her groom, when he walks down to meet her, she has been justified. This is her salvation from singleness to a married woman, and she takes on his name. On their wedding night they are sanctified to each other and become one as they consummate their marriage. As they grow and walk through life with difficult and adversities, they realize that their commitment to one another is everlasting until death. When death occurs, they will be glorified and see one another again.

---

[27] Ramm, Bernard, <u>Them He Glorified</u>, Wm. B. Eerdmans Publishing Company, Grand Rapids, Michigan, p61

Action points for the reader

1) Have you made a decision to accept the gift of salvation from God?

2) Have you come to an assurance of your personal salvation?

3) What changes do you see in your life as a result of your salvation? What changes are you still making?

The New Path

Salvation is the beginning of our relationship with God. As we journey through that relationship, we need to fellowship with Him daily to know who He is. His justification gives us the opportunity to repent and be restored of our wrong doing. Through His sanctification He sets us apart to himself that we may fulfill our purpose on earth, and He prepares us for His glorification. We glorify Him by being led by the Holy Spirit, obeying all of His commands and fulfilling the purpose that He put us on this earth to do. Salvation is a gift from God received through faith, grace, repentance, restoration, sanctification and glorification.

Open your heart to God's gift of salvation. Come into a closer fellowship with him and experience the blessings He has for you.

Action points for the reader

1) Go back to the early entries in your journal. Have any of your perspectives changed as you moved through the book? If so, how?
2) As you walk this new path, do you see the world differently?
3) How has your relationship with others changed as a result of your journey?

Prayer of Salvation of Abundant Life

(If you have not yet asked God into your life, you can do so right now. Use this prayer as an example. He is waiting for your call.)

    Father, I thank you for sending your son Jesus Christ to this earth to die for my sin. You said in your word if I confess with my mouth the Lord Jesus and believe in my heart that God has raised him from the dead, I will be saved. You also said, "with the heart man believeth unto righteousness; and with the mouth confession is made unto salvation (Roman 10: 9-10)."

    Father I confess, and I repent of my sins and I ask that you come into my heart, come in to stay. I believe that Jesus Christ died as me for all of my past, present, and future sins and I can have ever lasting life even after death. Thank you for saving me today and writing my name and my spiritual birthday in the Book of Life.

Name_____

Spiritual Birthday_____

Biography of Prophet/Dr. Thereasa Ball

Prophet/Pastor Dr. Thereasa Ball operates in the prophetic deliverance anointing, Gift of Prophecy, Word of Knowledge and Word of Wisdom. She ministers together with her husband, Apostle Dr. Johnnie Ball at Christian Embassy Fellowship in Picayune, Ms. Dr. Ball has been the prophet of her church for 32 years. She touches lives everywhere she goes. God uses her to bring spiritual insight to his people.

Dr. Ball operates in the prophetic anointing of the Five Fold Ministry (Apostles, Prophets, Evangelists, Pastors, and Teachers- Ephesians 4:12). Dr. Ball is currently a retired Day Care owner for 22 years. She assists her husband in ministering to drug/alcohol recovering addicts, backsliders and unsaved people. She is the Director of the women's ministry of Christian Embassy Fellowship. She is a Worshiper, Praise and Warrior, and a Seer for the Body of Christ. God uses her in dreams, visions and interpretations.

Dr. Ball is the mother of seven beautiful children and eight wonderful grandchildren, committed and submitted to her husband, Dr. Johnnie Ball. She is sold out to the Lord, walks in obedience to Jesus The Christ, and has made Him Lord of her life.

Dr. Ball wrote *The Journey of Abundant Life* because she wanted everyone to experience this pathway journey so that they would have life eternal with God and his Precious Son, Jesus the Christ.

Bibliography

Beall, James Lee, Pastor and Marjorie Barber, Laying The Foundation, (Bridge Publishing, Inc. South Plainfield, New Jersey, 1976).

Dawn Bible Students Association, Topical Bible Study, God's Plan for Man, Lesson VI, The Glory of the Terrestrial., Sept. 1961, (dawnbible.com/1961/6109tbs2.htm),East Rutherford, NJ.

Evans, Tony, Theology You Can Count On, Moody Publishes, Chicago, IL, 2008.

Evans, Tony, Totally Saved, Moody Publishers, Chicago, IL, 2002.

Finney, Charles G., Rev, Finney's Systematic Theology, 1878 Edition, Gospel Truth Ministries, Tustin, CA, 1966, Lecture 37, Sanctification

George, Elizabeth, Following God With All Your Heart, Growth and Study Guide, Harvest House Published by Harvest House Publishers, Eugene, Oregon 97402.

Killinger, John, The Changing Shape Of Our Salvation, The Crossroad Publishing Company, New York, NY, 2007.

MacDonald, William, What The Bible Teaches, (Emmanus Correspondence School, Dubuque, Iowa), 1976.

Price, Paula A. PH.D., The Prophet's Dictionary, Whitaker House, New Kensington, PA. 15068.

Ramm, Bernard, Them He Glorified, Wm. B. Eerdmans Publishing Company, Grand Rapids, Michigan.

Ryken, Philip Graham, The Message of Salvation, Minister of Tenth Presbyterian Church, Philadelphia, Pennsylvania.

Ryrie, Charles Caldwell, A Survey Of The Bible Doctrine, (The Moody Bible Institute of Chicago, 1972).

Ryrie, Charles C., So Great Salvation , Moody Publishers, Chicago, Ill., 1997.

Thiessen, Henry Clarence, Lectures In Systematic Theology, Wm. B. Eerdmans Publishing Co., Grand Rapids, Michigan, 2006.

Unger, Merrill F., The New Unger's Bible Dictionary, Revised and updated edition, The Moody Bible Institute of Chicago, Ill., 1988.

Vine, W.E., The Expanded Vines Expository Dictionary of New Testaments Words, (England by Oliphants, Marshall Pickering, 1940).

Webster, Merriam Inc., Webster's Ninth New Collegiate Dictionary, Springfield, Massachusetts, 1983).

Wilson, Neil S., The Handbook of Bible Application, Tyndale House Publishers, 1992.

Young, Douglas G, Young's Bible Dictionary, Tyndale's House Publishers, Inc., 1989.

Wikipedia, The Free Encyclopedia ,(en.wikipedia.org/wiki/glorification), p. 3

www.ingramcontent.com/pod-product-compliance
Lightning Source LLC
Chambersburg PA
CBHW060348050426
42449CB00011B/2882